The Diary of a Grieving Mother

SARAH BOULTON

"You Are My Sunshine" lyrics by Jimmie
Davis and Charles Mitchell.

"The Curious Case of Benjamin Button"
Dir. David Fincher, Warner Brothers 2008.

"How I Met Your Mother"
Carter Bays & Craig Thomas, CBS 2005.

"Harry Potter and the Prisoner of Azkaban"
J.K. Rowling, New York: Scholastic 1999.

"Jumanji: Welcome to the Jungle"
Dir. Jake Kasdan, Sony Pictures 2017.

"Jumanji: The Next Level"
Dir. Jake Kasdan, Sony Pictures 2019.

ACKNOWLEDGMENTS

Special thanks to:

Memaw, Nana, and Grandma.

The best grandmothers my kids could have. Thanks for your encouragement and for always telling me I should write a book.

And all the bereaved mothers I've leaned on since:

We find our strength in each other, knowing we are not alone in our pain. Acting as Aaron and Hur, we hold up one another's arms when we feel weak, reminding one another that God is with us.

YOU ARE MY SUNSHINE

You are my sunshine

My only sunshine

You make me happy

When skies are grey

You'll never know dear

How much I love you

Please don't take my sunshine away

The other night dear

As I lay sleeping

I dreamt I held you

Here in my arms

When I awoke dear

I was mistaken

So, I hung my head and cried

FOREWORD

I have always been chatty. When I was a kid, I would get in trouble at school for talking in class. My mom has frequently told me that I share too much and that I should practice being more reserved. No offense to my beautiful mother, but I feel like God gave me the gift of gab for a reason. I love talking. I love telling people funny stories about the truth of pregnancy and postpartum. I feel revived when I'm able to put into words how deeply I feel about God or my marriage or even how much I struggle with mental illness. I am moved deeply by the way people respond to the mental images that I am able to bring to life through words. In my short thirty-two years of life, I've made people laugh and cry and feel seen with my stories, sad, uncomfortable, or embarrassing as they were.

When I tell the story of how I met my husband, it isn't just a story of boy meets girl and then they get married and live happily ever after. There are years and years of intertwining subplots that led us to each other, revealing God's majesty and his ultimate plan to bring Spencer and I together... and there was more than just "happily ever after" for us afterwards, too. So why is our grief story only supposed to be five chapters? Shock, denial, anger, depression, acceptance? The story of losing our daughter is so much more than "she was stillborn." It's our whole story leading up to her death, and for many months afterward. It didn't end when she was gone. It didn't end once we had accepted her death. It still hasn't ended. Who knows if it ever will?

I invite you to read the story of our Kate, the full, unabridged story of grief and moving forward, even when your feet feel like lead.

BEFORE KATE

OUR BEGINNING

I'll spare the years-spanning story of how we met, and just tell you this: after spending one night out with this man, I knew I was destined to marry him. After our first date, he revealed the feeling was mutual. Our relationship developed very quickly, getting engaged less than six months later, and married less than eight months after that. My husband Spencer is a very practical, down-to-earth, patient, and gentleman. He is and has been my very best friend since day one. He's the only man gentle enough to handle my mood swings and anxiety, while still able to tactfully roast me the very moment my mood lightened. He's the first person I want to share funny videos with, and the last person I want to hug before going to bed.

We got married in November of 2015 and immediately after moved in with my parents.

Marine Corps housing took a while to find us a place to live, but come January, we had our little two-bedroom home on Camp Pendleton. When we learned that Spencer was going to deploy on a Marine Expeditionary Unit (MEU), we decided to make the most of this opportunity. We'd always planned to move to Oregon, where Spencer grew up after he got out of the service. So, this gave me and our new puppy, Bitty, an opportunity to move in with his family, save up some money, and get settled in the Pacific Northwest before his deployment ended. Upon the completion of his MEU, he returned to Southern California to complete his contract with the Marine Corps. We made trips to see each other at every opportunity until he finally came to be with me at his parent's home in Oregon in November of 2017.

MISCARRIAGE

In April of 2018, Spencer and I moved out of his parents' house and into our own apartment. This meant something huge for us: We could finally start trying for kids. As I got off birth control, we began to face some unexpected fertility issues and were very discouraged for a while. Not only that, but we realized that in some ways, this was our first time really living independently—it was like starting over in marriage. We'd spent the better part of a year apart after being married for less than a year previously. Looking back, I can say that the stress of our new dynamic was probably a contributing factor.

We made it through that first year in our way-too-cramped apartment and bought our beautiful house in May of 2019. We'd only been there a few weeks when I saw the plus sign I'd hoped so long to see. We'd heard that you should wait to tell your friends and family roughly twelve weeks, but we were too excited to wait. We'd called our parents, our siblings, our grandparents, told our coworkers, our closest friends. We were over the moon! We've made it through the rough years of marriage, we've bought a home, and we're having a baby! Nothing could bring us down. Not two weeks later, we were packing up the last few boxes of our apartment when I noticed I was bleeding. I told Spencer that it was probably nothing, a lot of women have light spotting in the first trimester. The next day, on May 26th, 2019, I woke up and the bleeding hadn't stopped.

When we got to the hospital, I told the receptionist my symptoms and hoped for the best. I was incredibly discouraged when the nurse saw us immediately, especially when there were quite a few other people ahead of us in the emergency room. They performed an ultrasound, and the ultrasound tech said something that I could only describe as a verbal slap-in-the-face. "We can't see that you were ever pregnant." I had taken five pregnancy tests, each saying positive. I don't understand. After an additional transvaginal ultrasound, I went to use the restroom, and I saw what I needed to see. I'd deluded myself for hours following, saying I hadn't seen what I thought I had seen. Maybe I was miraculously pregnant with twins and the other survived. Maybe that wasn't the baby at all, maybe the baby was still in there. I'd imagined girl names, maybe if I come up with a boy name, God will save my baby. Josiah! Josiah! I'll call him Josiah! He has a name, so you can't take him now! Just please don't tell me this is it! At the time, I thought this was the worst pain I would ever experience.

We decided to try again, and two months later, I got another positive test. This time, I waited two weeks to even tell Spencer that I was expecting. I surprised him in the parking lot, waiting for our first ultrasound. I'd convinced him that we were there for a "medical follow-up" after the miscarriage, and then moments before walking in, I told him we were actually there to see our new baby.

We went in for my induction on a Monday evening at exactly forty weeks pregnant. I slowly creeped into labor until early the next morning, and we quickly realized that epidurals don't exactly do much when you're experiencing back labour. Not sure what to expect in delivery, I ended up pushing for nearly four hours before he was finally ready to make an entrance. On March 31st, 2020, after twenty hours of gruelling labor, my Jack was finally here. By this point, nearly a year after the fact, I'd kind of justified that the baby I'd called Josiah died so I could have my Jack. It was easier to move on that way. I proudly called myself a "Rainbow Mama" and my little Jack my "Rainbow Baby." It had been such a short-lived period of grief before we were celebrating again. All the pain was seemingly forgotten, or at least swept under the rug.

SURPRISE

When Jack was about nine months old, we'd decided to try for a second child. It took us some time to get pregnant, but seven months later, we got the exciting news we'd been hoping for. I'd recently lost a friend to suicide, and as an homage to her, I'd scheduled to get some florals on my arm tattooed to honor her legacy as a woman chasing after Jesus. As I was sitting through the tattoo, though, I started to feel nauseated. I remember thinking how odd that was. I went home and decided to take a pregnancy test, just in case. I remember the digital test sitting on the counter, as my phone recorded it calibrating. I'd said, "Spencer and I have been trying to get pregnant for about nine months now..." When I'd finally glanced down at the test, I was in shock and elation to finally, after so long, read the word "Pregnant."

CURVEBALL

I'd had a fairly difficult first (and second, and third) trimester, with severe GERD, anemia, and morning sickness. I'd also contracted Covid-19, which caused me to lose fifteen pounds due to heightened nausea and parosmia. Having what I thought to be a miserable pregnancy with Jack, I was hoping this one would be easier. I got so unbelievably sick I didn't know how I was going to survive. Thankfully, not too long after, I was nearing the second trimester and nausea had subsided enough, so by Thanksgiving, Spencer and I were ready to tell the world: "We are EXTRA thankful this year!"

In January of 2022, I was roughly twenty weeks pregnant and eager to find out the sex of our baby. When we were pregnant with Jack, we'd had two names picked out: Violet Leona for a girl, and Jack Leon for a boy, (after my late grandfather, "Grandpa Leon"). When we'd discovered that our son was, in fact, a boy, my husband suggested that if we had a daughter in the future, we could still use the name Violet, but after one too many references to a certain children's movie, I was no longer interested in the name. Spencer was so frustrated with my "fickle" behavior that he decided we wouldn't even TALK about baby names until we knew the gender of this baby. So, there was a lot of excitement and anticipation regarding the gender reveal.

Since we were still amidst the Covid-19 pandemic, I had to go alone to the doctor's office. We'd decided that since my appointment was on Friday, I'd go in on Saturday to order the gender reveal cake, celebrate my birthday that evening, and then on Sunday, we'd pick up the cake and celebrate with my in-laws at their house. When I'd gotten to the doctor's office, I was so excited to see our baby, to turn thirty, and to have our gender reveal celebration. All of that came to a screeching halt when I was taken aside to be told that they found something in the ultrasound. I will never forget the doctor who very bluntly stated that my child had a valve stenosis, that she would likely not make it to delivery, and that "most women in this position consider an abortion." This news had cast a shadow over what should have been an exciting, wonderful weekend. By Sunday evening, we were completely discouraged, almost not even wanting to partake in our own gender reveal, but that dark shadow disappeared in an instant when we saw the pink icing. We're having a girl.

We'd spent the next week doing a ton of research (and bitterly hoping that Doctor What's-Her-Face would break her ankle), when we found that most of what we'd been told was the absolute worst-case scenario. Best case scenario: her heart heals completely. Most likely, however, was that she'd be carried to term, have a short NICU stay, and then have open heart surgery to correct the stenosis, but otherwise have a long and healthy life. As time went on, we were more and more hopeful and trusted that God would either heal her heart or that she'd thrive after surgery. When I'd seen the pediatric cardiologist, he told me that her heart had started to heal, but only partly. He said that she would be carried to term, be delivered in the NICU in Portland, and then have surgery at two months old. We can do this.

KICKING

I remember sitting in my rocking chair downstairs, feeling her wiggle and kick on a Wednesday evening. We'd finally decided on a first name a month earlier, and a middle name two weeks later. We were torn between two names: Casey and Kate. Spencer and I jokingly asked the baby to pick. We said, "Casey... Casey... Casey..." and she was quiet. But when Spencer said, "Kate," she kicked. "Kate." She kicked again. We loved Amelia for a first name, but our friends had just named their daughter Amelia, so we chose Amelia for the middle name. Kate "Katie" Amelia. She was always kicking: when I sang, when Jack laughed, when Spencer talked to her. So, it was very odd that Thursday afternoon when I realized that I hadn't felt her move in a while. I reasoned with myself that it was just a result of nesting; I'd been cooking, cleaning and running around the house. Maybe she was just being moved around too much for her to want to wiggle and kick. By the next morning, I knew something was wrong. I told Spencer to watch Jack, I would run to the doctor's, in my pajamas, get a quick Doppler test to confirm that she's fine and just getting ready for delivery, and I'd be home in an hour or two—just in time for Spencer to head to work.

Immediately after arriving at the Women's Health Center, I was told I needed to meet my doctor in the Labor and Delivery unit of the main hospital. After taking my blood pressure and doing the usual tests, they did the Doppler test, and immediately sent for an ultrasound machine. After another two ultrasounds, my doctor confirmed that my greatest fear in this pregnancy had come true. There was no heartbeat. Our Kate was gone.

AFTER KATE

THE FIRST WAVE

"God, how could you do this to me?"

"I had BOLD FAITH, God, I had BOLD
FAITH!"

"What did I do wrong, God??"

"Jesus, please!"

"Why, God, why?"

I had the nurses call Spencer to tell him to
make his way to the hospital. I learned later that
they had only told him that there was a
complication, they wanted him to hear it from
me. He walked in with panic on his face, asking
what was going on. He came over to me as I
laid on the hospital bed and tearfully asked, "Is
she gone?" How do you tell your best friend,
the love of your life, that his daughter is dead?

We held each other and cried for what seemed like an eternity.

Spencer had dropped Jack off at a neighbor's house and called his mom to pick him up and keep him for as long as we were at the hospital. We called her back once she was back at her house to let her know what had happened. I called my mom and dad who were already making their way up to see us—they'd planned to road trip to be here for the birth and stay with us for a month to help us out with the new baby—they had to pull over at the next truck stop to cry. We called Spencer's dad and stepmom and asked them if they would want to drive down from Spokane to see us at the hospital. Lastly, we called Spencer's aunt and uncle, who have been like an extra set of parents to us. We texted our friends copied and pasted messages just stating what happened and asking for prayer.

LAUGHING, I GUESS?

I couldn't tell you why, but I must've turned into the designated Labor and Delivery Unit comedian that day. In between bouts of sobbing so hard I couldn't see, I was making the nurses laugh. It was such a weird place to be. Complete shock, devastation, denial, confusion, anger, and laughter? I shouldn't be laughing. I shouldn't be making dirty jokes, winking at my husband like I don't have a dead child in my stomach. I'd walk to the bathroom, look at my huge belly, thinking, *she's in there, but she's gone,* come back, crack a joke about my "fall risk" socks that had everyone in stitches, watch the nurses walk away and break down crying again. I've always used humor to cope. This time, though, it felt wrong—distasteful, insensitive—even though I couldn't seem to stop making jokes, trying to make people laugh. Looking back I can definitely see that it was just my subconscious trying to replace the pain with something funny, like using the "ridikulus" charm from Harry Potter.

When we were in the hospital with our miscarriage almost exactly three years prior, we were left in the room alone for several hours, just waiting for various things. We'd decided to kill some time and watch the new Jumanji. We ended up loving the movie, so when we saw Jumanji 2 while we were in the hospital with Kate, we figured it was nostalgic in the worst way, so obviously we had to watch it. The movie gave an ending that seemed to imply there would be a third installment, to which both of us said we better not be back here watching Jumanji 3.

Once Spencer arrived at the hospital the doctors gave me my first (and only) dose of Misoprostol, which started the long labor process. Thankfully my body took over and there was no need for Pitocin. The epidural went beautifully, and I was in absolutely no pain during the entire labor and delivery. After pushing for exactly three minutes, she was here. The silence in the room weighed so heavily on my heart. Spencer told me later that he was secretly hoping that she'd somehow miraculously be revived and start crying once she was in my arms. We each held her and wept. Spencer later told me that he regretted holding her and looking at her that way. He wanted to remember her as her ultrasound photo, her kicking, the beautiful life in my belly. He gently reminded me that, "This is not our daughter. Our daughter is in Heaven with her Savior. This is only her body."

My doctor gave us permission to go home that night so we'd invited our parents to take turns to come to the hospital to meet our sweet girl and say goodbye, and then we would pick up our son and drive home. My parents were the last to arrive. They helped Spencer load up the car and walked us out. Spencer, being the angel that he is, had removed the infant car seat from the back seat of our little Toyota and put it in the trunk. He said he knew how hard it would be to see it empty on the drive home.

We'd loaded up the car and sat down for a moment, and in the silence that should have been filled with a cooing baby girl, we both began to sob. Spencer has never been a big crier. He's only cried a handful of times in our ten years together. I think nothing is as disheartening as to watch your rock, your best friend, your hero, completely inconsolable. This was a pain I couldn't fix, and all I wanted to do was make it better for him, even though I was in it too, just as deep.

But then, Jack.

We had arrived at my in-laws' house to pick up our then two-year-old son, Jack, got him buckled in, and as we were both preparing to resume crying, Jack started laughing. Not genuine laughter, but a very goofy, very loud, forced laugh. "Ha. Ha. Ha." Since he was about a year old, he's had this hilarious "practice laugh." It's literally as if he's just practicing how to laugh and it's so fake and so precious and so silly. His goofy practice laugh had us in stitches. We looked at each other then and Spencer said,

"If we ever only get to raise one beautiful child, we have one beautiful child." We have said many times that I think our saving grace in this grief is that our Jack brings us so much joy. At that moment, it didn't feel wrong to laugh. It felt like a hot desert getting a cool rain: incredibly refreshing and exactly what we needed.

WHAT IS GRIEF

"What are you supposed to do when your daughter dies? We've gotten flowers, meals, and donations to help us financially. We've gotten keepsakes, and a plan for her ashes.

"But as life calls us to go back into routine more and more, what do we do? It's not like a breakup where there's a typical formula: mani/pedis, get your hair done, go shopping, change your Facebook status and have a girls' night out. You see it in all the movies, you read it in the books.

"But there's no formula, no routine, no guided plan to get you through the death of a child, to get you through the long drive home from the hospital, when you're expecting to have a cooing baby in the backseat and instead it's just silent except for the sounds of quiet sobs coming from mom and dad. Nothing to prepare you for when you see her crib made up with her llama stuffy, and breakdown because you were so excited to give it to her and watch her grow up with it. Nothing to tell you about how every night you and your husband take turns snuggling with the blanket that she was wrapped in.

"Our only thoughts are just "how to survive today," not even "what would make me feel better," simply "what will keep me alive." Don't get me wrong, I'd like to do the mani/pedis and go to the hair salon, and I might later, but right now my plan for today consists of taking care of Jack, eating at least two meals, and going back to bed, maybe I'll cry sometime today, if I have the energy.

"I usually like to end posts like this with an optimistic turn or biblical encouragement. And while I know that God is always good and that we'll get through this, I don't have it in me to pretend that I'm okay right now."

—From Sarah's Instagram

We all know the five stages of grief—denial, anger, bargaining, depression, and acceptance—but the question we always hear is, "Will it ever go away?" The simple answer is no. To kind of explain our weird mood swings during our stay at the hospital, I referred to this metaphor. Imagine for me, if you will, one of those yellow, one-inch, rubber bouncy balls bouncing off the walls inside a small box. Every time the bouncy ball hits a button on the side of the box, a buzzer goes off, and there is a pang of grief, whether it's a sigh of discouragement or a full-blown meltdown in the middle of a nail salon with waterworks and questioning, "Why, God?" (A completely fake scenario that absolutely never ever happened, probably.) Three things are constant: the color of the ball, the speed at which it moves—it never slows down, never stops—and the shape and size of the ball. The only thing that will change is the size of the box, which is slowly growing. (You can never change what happened, you can't find a way for it to hurt less than it does, and you cannot control how frequently you feel it, but life and time continue on.) At first, the box is so small, the size of a child's shoe box, this bouncy ball can't go more than just a few moments without setting off the buzzer. Over time, though, the box will grow to the size of a cardboard packing box, then the size of a small room, then the size of a house, then the size of a warehouse, and so on and so forth. It'll get to a point where it's been so long since it set off the buzzer, and you'll think it's over, but it's still moving. It's moving at the exact same pace it was moving when it started. You'll never be "over it," and you'll never be done grieving, but those pangs get farther apart, allowing for life to take place in between those moments.

BOLD FAITH

Let me start this off by saying:

GOD IS NOT A VENDING MACHINE.

For Christmas of 2021, I asked my mom for a Passionate Penny Pincher planner. With the planner, she also got me the set of journals for the New Testament reading plan. I don't do reading plans, especially since the Bible in a year plan is a lot more than my ADHD brain can handle. BUT! I decided that come January first I could read through the New Testament in a year. Everywhere you look in the Gospels, God is calling his people to bold faith, then Jesus calls his disciples to bold faith. I've gotten to the point of writing "BOLD FAITH" next to every passage with this message. If it's mentioned so frequently, it must be important. What does bold faith look like? As you know, three weeks into this new venture of mine, reading one chapter every weekday, we got the news about Kate's heart condition. So I took it upon myself to practice bold faith, which in hindsight was somewhat akin to Aladdin tricking the Genie into getting him out of the cave.

I prayed:

"God, you are so great and powerful, I know you'll heal Kate's heart..."

"God, it would be so easy for you to heal Kate's heart, I know you will heal her..."

"In Jesus' name, her heart will be healed..."

"God, I know you won't do this to us. I know that we'll have a happy, healthy baby girl..."

"Thank you, Jesus, for healing her heart like I know you can..."

"...but not my will but yours be done."

I'm embarrassed about it now, though what else is a mother to do when she's faced with the thought of losing her child or watching as her child endures open heart surgery at only a few days old? Truthfully, I still don't understand bold faith. I don't know how to do it, or what to pray for. Our old church used to always say, "The way God dealt with people then is the way God deals with people now," referring to how they had the word and the holy spirit the same way we do. Miracles are still happening, they haven't stopped. We've just become so "do it yourself" that we don't recognize them as miracles anymore. But if that's the case, and I truly believed that God is good, that God does miracles, and that God would allow us to raise our daughter, then why did she die? I asked my mom this one day and she told me that maybe the bold faith is simply trusting that whatever happens, God is still good.

FALLEN WORLD

I know a lot of people who have endured hardship, loss, or what have you, who've decided that God wasn't with them, wasn't good or wasn't real. "If God is real and he loves us and he's good, why does he let people die?" Seems like a reasonable question if you don't consider that there is an enemy among us. We forget that we live in a fallen world, where the enemy runs rampant. We forget that this world belongs to him. We forget that even in times where our country or household is at peace, there is a spiritual war between Heaven and Hell for your soul. The enemy will do anything in his power to keep you from believing in God, and because he, like us, has free will, that means that sometimes awful things happen. I think of it like a game of chess. God offers up his knight for the enemy's pawn to take. "How foolish," he thinks. "God is just GIVING me his pieces." All the while, God's on the other side of the board, setting up his queen to take the enemy's king, and by moving his pawn, the enemy has just cleared a path.

When we lost Kate, a lot of people said things like "God needed her more than you did," or "maybe it's a blessing in disguise." What. A. LIE! I didn't doubt that God would use this for his glory, or that maybe because of this grief I would receive another miracle later in life, but this just a terrible thing to say to someone who is grieving. What a weird way to invalidate my pain! Don't get me wrong, everyone who offered any kind of encouragement was greatly appreciated and deeply loved by us, but these things simply weren't true. It wasn't a blessing. God did not "need" her. She isn't an angel now. We simply need to accept that sometimes terrible things happen, but in the book of John, Chapter Eleven, we read that God grieves with us. Even if he's got a plan to make a masterpiece of our mess, he still mourns with us.

SO, SO LOVED

Of all the things that could possibly come from this grief, the first and foremost would be the incredible outpour of love that we received in the days and weeks following her death. Once word got out to our friends and families, we couldn't go five minutes without a new message, phone call, like, comment, or share. One of our concerns was that, aside from our emergency savings account, we weren't going to have income if Spencer took time off work. We were relying on him getting paid parental leave for two weeks and then him taking another two weeks off to help with Kate and get to know her. When she passed away, we were not given a birth certificate because legally, she was never alive. That meant that Spencer could not take paid parental leave. He was instead offered three days paid bereavement and permitted to take the month off with a promise of a job when he was ready to return. A friend of ours decided to set up a GoFundMe for us, so we could pay for our bills without having to empty our savings account. She set the goal for $4,500, roughly a month's worth of income, and between the GoFundMe and people giving to us directly, we exceeded our goal by a long shot. We were also blessed with gorgeous bouquets, heartfelt letters, home-cooked meals, grocery and fast-food deliveries, coloring books for Jack, books about grief, and personalized keepsakes.

I don't say this to brag, but rather to share how deeply loved we are. I am near tears as I'm remembering how much people went out of their way to show us they cared and that we were not alone. I told Spencer's uncle that I felt like there was a small army of people praying for us. He very gently stated, "It's not small. You've got people quite literally all over the world who are praying for you." I'd never felt so comforted, so loved, so not-alone. To say that we were beyond blessed by everyone who came together to take care of us in any and every way is a gross understatement. And to think, we probably would not have felt the magnitude of God's love like this had we not first gone through the loss.

FALSE HOPE

"Back in January, when I was around twenty-two weeks pregnant, I went to get the anatomy scan done for our baby. Before we even knew if it was a boy or a girl, they told us that there was a heart condition. The (very indelicate) doctor who delivered the news said that there was a risk of stillbirth. We were so terrified, and it put a dark cloud over the gender reveal and my birthday (that same weekend). A few weeks later, we saw a cardiologist who corrected the previous statement by saying that this type of heart condition was not deadly in any way, but that she would probably need surgery, or she'd have trouble breathing. We felt such a huge relief, and we celebrated our little girl, all the way up until she stopped moving. They assured us that her death had nothing to do with the heart condition, the umbilical cord, or trauma of any sort. But we still lost her.

"I wondered why our all-knowing God allowed us to have this false hope, when we'd already been (falsely) warned of a stillbirth. Why didn't he take her then, before our hopes were lifted and we were assured a happy and healthy baby girl? Or why did the doctors celebrate the insignificance of her heart condition instead of being cautious and reserved? The only answer I can come up with is that maybe he knew we needed the extra joy. We needed the delight of having a daughter. Maybe he wanted my heart to make room for her so we'd want to try again when she didn't make it earthside.

"I keep saying that when we get pregnant again, I don't think it'll hurt as badly, because we wouldn't have this other child if we hadn't lost Kate. But we're not there yet. And we don't know what the future brings, if we will even be able to have another child.

"All I know is that I loved Kate. I don't regret the hope we were given. I don't regret the extra time, so to speak. She got to pick out her name, hear her brothers laugh, kick dada's hand, and listen to mama sing. Maybe it wasn't for us, that she went full term. Maybe it was for her. Maybe she's in heaven telling Jesus about her family. Maybe."

—From Sarah's Instagram

CRUEL IRONY

During my entire pregnancy, I had GERD, which caused me to cut out most seasonings, anything too spicy, too sweet, too acidic, too carbonated, et cetera. Essentially, I had to cut out anything with flavor. I even had to switch my choice of bottled water to alkaline. In doing so, I managed to not gain a lot of weight in my pregnancy like I had with Jack. In fact, I didn't gain any. When we got home from the hospital and I'd taken a shower, I looked at my body in the mirror and thought how, even at a few days postpartum, I felt more attractive than I had before even being pregnant with Kate.

When I was in the hospital with Jack, I'd experienced severe back labor that the epidural couldn't seem to touch. It had gotten to the point of asking for an extra epidural whenever it was available to me. This caused a myriad of postpartum difficulties, including having a really hard time walking for a few days afterward because I was so weak from the pain and still could not feel my legs. I'd been on an IV for so long with Jack that my face, hands, and feet all began to swell and to be honest, I felt like my most unattractive self in those first few pictures with my son. With Kate, however, the epidural worked so beautifully that I was able to sleep most of the night, and was half asleep when the doctors told me it was time to start pushing, and she was here within three minutes, versus the four hours of (premature) pushing it took to bring Jack into this world.

I got home and while they'd prescribed me the usual painkillers, I didn't feel the need to take them. I was able to move freely, sleep comfortably, shower safely, all within seven hours of delivering my daughter. I experienced no severe cramping, no pain, no physical weakness whatsoever. To top it all off, the extra pregnancy weight seemed to fall off with minimal effort. Oh, and my breastmilk came in full force very quickly, whereas with Jack, it was an emotionally gruelling experience. I frequently thought how this would have been the perfect postpartum experience... if only I'd actually gotten to keep my girl.

To be honest, this felt like a cruel irony. It brought back memories of moving to Oregon during the coldest and most brutal winter they'd had in about five years, and have had since. The week we arrived in Oregon, as we'd prepared to send Spencer off to deployment, it rained and rained and rained, cold and miserable. However, the day I dropped him off at the airport and said "goodbye" to my brand-new husband, it was sunny and warm. Of course. It felt like cruel irony. It felt like God was laughing at me. "I'm going to give you exactly what you want, but in the circumstance you absolutely won't be able to enjoy it in." So when I came out of the hospital feeling healthy, beautiful, and strong, the feeling came rushing back. "Here's exactly what you wanted, but good luck enjoying it."

Looking back, I think that maybe God was trying to give me an ounce of relief. Maybe the sunshine and warmth were supposed to be a "bright side" when my heart was heavy. Maybe my health and self-image were boosted so I could relieve an ounce of the heartache I'd experienced losing Kate. I wish I could have seen it that way then.

ASHES TO ASHES

"What do we do with her body?" I wish no parent ever had to ask this question. It's not like we could ask her, "Hey, I know you're just now able to wiggle your toes in utero, but I wanted to ask—what you want us to do with your body after you die?" We decided not to do an autopsy, we didn't want to know. Or maybe we did, but the thought of taking several months to get back to us with the information wasn't something we looked forward to. Spencer and I said that if it would help the hospital to learn more or possibly prevent a stillbirth for someone else in the future, then it would be worth it, but the doctors told us that at this point it would only be for our benefit. We decided it wasn't worth it. It couldn't bring her back. We did eventually find out, but more on that later. We were hoping that we would be able to donate her organs, but by the time she was delivered she'd been gone for about two days. She was too far gone for her death to help another child.

We hadn't thought much about burial because the thought of having a funeral was too painful to bear. We were told that there was a funeral home in our area that did free cremations for infants. Since free was affordable, we decided to go there to have her cremated. But even if we had her cremated, what would we do with her ashes? We thought of our options, an urn, scattering them, even putting them in epoxy to make a paperweight or something. None of them felt right. None of them felt like what we should do with our daughter. She wasn't given a chance at life, so I didn't want to just keep her on my shelf. If we'd scattered her ashes at Crown Point, one of our favorite spots in Oregon, then we'd be apart from her forever. The idea of making her ashes into a paperweight gave my parents the heebie-jeebies, so what next?

A few days after her passing, we'd set up a Facetime with Spencer's aunt, Sarah, and uncle, Peter, in California. They had told us about how when Sarah's mother passed, they took her hair and had it turned into a diamond, and that they could do the same with ashes. We loved this idea! But man, it was so expensive. We were relying on our friends and family to help us just to cover our bills, we couldn't imagine how we'd afford this process. That's when Peter said the unimaginable, "If you would like to turn Kate's ashes into a diamond, we'd be happy to pay for it." What!? Instantly, Spencer and I broke down sobbing. We were just amazed at their generosity for the perfect way to put our beautiful girl to rest. We thought about our options for a while and then settled on the idea of our little girl being transformed into a beautiful pink diamond.

When we went to pick up her ashes, we were expecting a long, awkward conversation with the woman who ran the funeral home, but she was refreshingly brief in handing us our daughter... in a small cardboard box. It was so small. It wasn't even big enough to hold my iPhone 11... and this is all we have of our daughter? Spencer and I walked to our car and sat there for a few moments, tearing up and saddened by the smallness of what was left of our baby. I couldn't tell you why, but I hugged the box. When we got home, I did what I said I didn't want to do and set her on the shelf.

We were told that to start the diamond process they needed a certain amount of ash, and we were concerned that we wouldn't have enough, but we remembered that Sarah had said that she'd also added her hair and their son's hair to supplement. We decided to do the same with ours. We debated whether or not to use Jack's hair, namely because if we had another child, that child might feel left out, but Spencer told me that he wanted it to be our little family, and if we have another child and ask why they weren't a part of it, we'll simply say "because you weren't here yet!" So Spencer and I got haircuts, bringing our hair home in little bags. We'd taken Jack to get a haircut around Christmas time, and my mom decided that since it was the first time he didn't cry for a haircut, that they should keep some of his hair from his "real first haircut." I'm glad for my sentimental mother because we were able to use that hair to add to our collection.

When my parents made the road trip back to California, they took her with them. As bummed as I was to see them go, I think saying goodbye to Kate hurt worse.

BECAUSE

"I guess yesterday was rainbow baby day. As many of you know, Kate wasn't our first loss. Back in 2019 we suffered a miscarriage two months before Jack was conceived. I realize that in addition to our sweet Jack, if we are able to conceive again, that child will also be a rainbow baby.

"It's a weird (and rather discouraging) thought that we only get to raise one of our three children. It's really made me question if we'll even be successful in trying to have another child.

"What's interesting is in a lot of cases, when people say "rainbow baby" they mean the child that came after the loss. But I think in our case any child we're blessed to raise would be a rainbow in the sense that they happened because of the loss. If we'd had our first child, we would not have had Jack. We had planned to stop trying for children after Kate was born, so any child we have moving forward will only be because we lost Kate. I think that thought gives me hope in knowing that if we are able to conceive, I won't be bitter from the storm because it brought me a beautiful rainbow.

"I don't know everything. All I know is that every day I pray that God will bring us another daughter, that we can have two beautiful rainbow babies. And that most of all, his will be done."

—From Sarah's Instagram

If you've seen <u>The Curious Case of Benjamin Button</u>, you'll hear about how if Daisy hadn't stopped for a moment to wait for her friend to tie her shoe, or this or that seemingly insignificant thing, she would not have been hit by the car, which ended her career as a ballerina and changed her life. If you've seen <u>How I Met Your Mother,</u> you know that Ted meets the mother because of the girl he met while teaching a class, which only happened because Tony gave him a job, and Tony only gave him a job because he'd dated Stella. He'd only met Stella because of the butterfly tattoo, he only got the butterfly tattoo because he was trying to "win the breakup with Robin," which only happened because back in 2007, he noticed her from across the bar. One small thing leads to a million bigger things.

With the baby I'd called Josiah, it was easy to just "move on" because we had Jack. I almost had to be thankful that we'd lost that baby because if he'd survived then we wouldn't have Jack. Sounds terrible, doesn't it? I'm so thankful for my son, so I have to be thankful for all the terrible things that came before. Every heartbreak, every stubbed toe, every failed test, every loss, including our miscarriage. When Kate passed, I couldn't justify it this way. I couldn't look at it like that at first because Kate could have survived delivery at that point, and we could have conceived another child and had both. But let's look at it this way. Let's imagine in the future, I get pregnant again and have a bouncy baby boy named Billy Bob McGee. (Please don't ever name your child Billy Bob McGee.) I had decided not to have another child after Kate, so if she'd survived, I would have missed out on Billy. If she'd survived and we chose to have another child, we would have probably wanted to wait longer to try again for another child, so we would have missed out on Billy. Now imagine we decided to jump the gun and try to get pregnant immediately after Kate was born, but Kate had a blowout at the grocery store, so I had to go home, give her a bath, put the kids to bed, and then I stayed up cleaning her car seat and doing laundry. I took a shower, but I still feel like I'm covered in baby poo, and I still haven't eaten dinner, and you know what, let's just have sex tomorrow. We would have missed. Out. On. Billy.

It's not always fun and not always easy, but looking at my grief through that lens, I have to see all the ways God can use this blowout diaper of a situation for the good of his kingdom. I'm writing this book, I met many new friends who've also lost children, and people have seen my faith thrive in this dark time... This could be my ministry. OR We could have another child, that child could grow up and get married one day, and their future grandchild could be the president of the United States. There are endless possibilities of what beautiful things God can make from this grief.

NEW NORMAL

It took quite a while for us to get back to normal again. Spencer finally went back to work on June 30th, about a week after my parents left. I got into a pretty good routine.

7:00 a.m.:	Spencer wakes up.
	Jack wakes up and plays in his room.
9:00 a.m.:	Time to wake up!
	I get Jack, make coffee and breakfast for the family.
	Jack watches TV and plays.
	Daddy relaxes.
12:00 p.m.:	Jack takes a nap.
	Spencer leaves for work.

	I read my bible, then read a book or take a nap.
3:00 p.m.:	Wake up Jack for lunch.
	I take Jack to run an errand, go to the park, or we watch Spanish nursery rhymes while I do chores.
7:00 p.m.:	Dinner time.
7:30 p.m.:	Bath time.
8:00 p.m.:	Jack's Bedtime.
	I do chores, shower, then read.
10:00 p.m.:	Spencer comes home from work
	We chat about his day and I get ready for bed while he unwinds downstairs.
12:00 a.m.:	Spencer and I go to sleep.

I can't stress this enough: routine is so important when it comes to grief. It's something to rely on even when your brain can't process what's happening. I look at the clock and think, "Oh it's time to take a nap, better take a nap... Oh, it's time to eat." It's hard enough getting out of bed on your own when you're grieving, but having this routine makes sure that, at the very least, we're taken care of. I frequently refer to Maslow's Hierarchy of Needs. I'm a psychology buff, so I love this stuff. Essentially, it prioritizes the various needs of a person. The most basic is food, water, and rest. Then shelter, safety, hygiene, and resources. Then, friendship, love, and a sense of belonging. Then self-esteem respect and freedom. The last is the desire to improve oneself. When you're in grief, you simply need to focus on your most basic needs: Eating, sleeping, and bathing.

We were in a sermon a few weeks ago talking about depression and anxiety and I really appreciated when the pastor said that taking medication is one of the simplest things you can do to help get you through a tough chapter. He said that no one with cancer would ever feel embarrassed to go to chemo, and no one with diabetes would be laughed at for taking insulin, so why should we feel embarrassment or shame when it comes to taking care of our mental health? Taking your medicine is meeting a basic need.

I also remembered learning about how trauma affects the brain when I was in college. Frequently, our brains will block out painful memories causing a lapse in memory, delusions, or in my case a very odd form of denial. Part of moving forward for me was consistently reminding myself what happened. For weeks, it felt like the nine-plus months hadn't happened. Or rather, they had, but I wasn't pregnant. I would look at selfies from Christmas and not register that I was pregnant in those photos. I would think back to Easter Sunday and imagine walking around in my easter dress with a flat belly, only to look back at pictures and realize I was almost eight months pregnant.

It was the oddest thing to walk around and feel the need to remind myself that I was pregnant and I did have a daughter, and that she is dead. Truthfully, it almost seemed like it was worse because instead of just having this knowledge in the back of my mind, I had to fight to keep those memories of her. I only have a few photos from that day and when we got home from the hospital, Spencer kindly asked me to not look at them when he's around. He said, "This isn't how I want to remember her... that wasn't my daughter, just her body." And while I can see where he's coming from, I needed to look at those photos almost every night to confirm that she was real, that this wasn't some bad dream I woke up from, that I had a daughter and lost a daughter.

COPING DIFFERENTLY

I love finding out my personality types: ENFJ, Orange in relationships, Blue in communication, Hufflepuff, Black Bear, Love languages are gifts and words, et cetera. Funnily enough, my husband hates these descriptors. He thinks we're just people and we don't need to be put in groups. But I've found that these descriptors have really helped the way I go about marriage.

Unfortunately, being a psychology enthusiast, I've heard about the statistics behind marriages that fall apart after the loss of a child, and truthfully, I wouldn't even want to talk about it if I didn't feel it was important to share. Remember this: the enemy will take any and every opportunity to destroy a healthy marriage, and a marriage overshadowed by grief is an easy target. The biggest reason for this is simple: we're different...and we cope differently. Now let me preface by stating that our marriage is and always has been wonderful, healthy, and stable, and it was never in danger of falling apart. I will say, however, that our differences in coping caused me to believe that maybe our marriage was in trouble.

Spencer had become withdrawn and started playing his video games more frequently. Normally, I don't mind as long as he's at least mostly present in the room, even if there's no conversation—I like to know that if I need help with Jack, or if I think of something important, that I can quickly get his attention. When he started playing again, he started wearing his noise-cancelling headphones while he was in Discord with his friends. We'd get into small, little bickering matches over this but nothing too major. Until one day I started feeling insecure, and I realized that he hadn't been very affectionate with me. In fact, he had been really quiet and not really wanting to talk to me either. I tend to spiral very quickly, and so my over-thinking, insecure mind quickly decided that he blamed me for our daughter's passing and was just doing what he could to avoid me. Our little bickering matches turned into full-blown meltdowns, leaving me scared of being left and my husband confused and concerned.

One day, my depression got so bad I called the county crisis hotline. The woman on the other end heard my story and very patiently explained that despite the months that had passed, we were still in grief, and it seems as though we're grieving differently. Spencer is an INTP in the Meyers-Briggs personality test, where I'm an ENFJ. INTPs are Introverted, Intuition, Thinking, and Perceiving. ENFJs are Extroverted, Intuition, Feeling, and Judging. For those who might not be familiar with these terms, my husband prefers to be alone, whereas I prefer to be around groups of people. He makes decisions based on logic, whereas mine are based on how I feel. He is slow to develop his opinion, whereas I'm quick to have an opinion and equally quick to change it later as necessary. I took this bit of information and went to the internet.

"How do INTP's grieve?" I asked Google. What I found caused me so much relief and embarrassment. INTPs like my husband prefer to withdraw from their friends and family. Frequently, they want to sort things out themselves before coming to someone else with their thoughts and feelings. Often feeling uncomfortable with the topic, they like to lose themselves in exercise, work, or in my husband's case, video games. What a grieving INTP needs most is space and time. Just for kicks, I also looked up how ENFJs grieve. ENFJs like myself prefer to see that other's needs are taken care of first, trying to maintain an image of being collected while inwardly falling apart—this explained my bizarre comic routine at the hospital. They later can become very critical of others, often lashing out harshly—this explained my daily meltdowns. What the grieving ENFJ needs most is affection and reassurance—this explained everything else.

It is no wonder we were fighting so much. When we finally sat down and talked about it, we saw that while each of us was still in grief, we needed to help the other person grieve too. I needed to be less critical when Spencer needed time alone, and Spencer needed to know that initiating affection was really important to me. If I could give couples advice on how to proceed after this kind of loss, I'd say to take the silly personality tests. Do your research, find out how people similar to your spouse cope with grief and what makes them feel loved, pick up on their habits and notice the changes. Be patient, and

"Above all, love each other deeply, because love covers over a multitude of sins."

—1 Peter 4:8 NIV

SHOULD WE? AND IF SO, WHEN?

When Jack was born, after twenty gruelling hours of labor, Spencer asked the age-old question every baby-crazy husband asks, "When do you want to do this again??" I could've ripped his head off. But when Kate passed away, that question didn't seem so awful. "Should we try again?" At first it was an "I'm not sure I can do this again." That evolved to "I want to try again but I am afraid to lose another child," which quickly became "I want to try again, but let's wait a few months to start trying." Finally, we decided "I'm pretty sure three weeks was long enough to heal, let's try now."

It's really hard to explain to people our desire to have another baby so quickly—unless they've been through this. A girlfriend of mine had gone through a similar experience, only getting to enjoy four days with her precious girl before surrendering her to her creator. She told me that after experience she came across a book entitled Empty Arms by Pam Vredevelt. She explained that losing a child feels like your arms are just empty, that you should be holding a newborn baby that you can't seem to put down, and not so empty. I would never want Kate to be looking down at us from heaven and thinking that she was "replaced" but at the same time, I was denied the pleasure of raising my beautiful daughter—is it wrong to want another chance?

When I was pregnant with Jack, I thought that I'd seen the worst of what pregnancy could be, and labor with him as exponentially worse. I was so traumatized by the whole ordeal that it took me a while to come to a place where I'd even consider trying again. Once we finally got pregnant with Kate, a new fear came up. What if I don't love this baby as much as I love Jack? What if Jack resents me for having another baby? Did we just ruin our lives by getting pregnant again? Once we found out she was a girl, we were so excited and it felt like the Grinch's heart growing three sizes. My heart grew and made room for this precious baby girl.

When she passed, it was like that space in my heart was not only empty but suffering. It was as if the hope of this daughter held the walls up of this new room. With the room being empty, the roof is caving in, the walls that were once strong with excitement and love are now damaged and compromised. It's not just this space that's in danger of falling apart, but the whole house... my whole heart. In desperate hope of a This Is Us type scenario, I not-so-jokingly asked the nurses if a baby had been dropped off that day. Not to replace my beautiful daughter, but to keep the roof from caving in.

I really sat for a while and thought about the difference between replacing her and having another child. It's hard to think of things to compare it to because there's nothing that compares to losing your child before you've gotten to meet them. I will never get to hear her laugh, I'll never know what color her eyes were, I'll never even get to see if she's ticklish, much less get to know the nuances in her character that make her who she is. All I had was a pregnancy. So if I have another child, am I replacing her?

I'm a chatty person, I've always been a little too open with people. I'm the lady you'll see chatting up the check stand employee, while the line is forming behind me. Frequently, I'll go to the store or the coffee shop with Jack and I'll strike up a conversation with the people around me. One of the most common questions I get is, "How many kids do you have?" Truth? I have no idea how to answer this question. My knee-jerk reaction is to say I have two. I had two full-term pregnancies, two deliveries, and held two babies. But that doesn't feel right, because now I'm leaving out Josiah. I was only four weeks along when I lost him. I don't even know if he was a boy or if she was a girl! I never saw his face, never held him in my arms. Do I say I have three children? Is that confusing or morbid? Or is it just uncomfortable for those around me to hear? "I have three kids, two of which are dead." Maybe I should say I have one child. Just Jack... but that feels wrong in a different way, like I'm lying or hiding from a painful truth. If I have another child, what will I say then? Two kids? Three? Four? These profoundly uncomfortable questions make me realize one undebatable truth:

Mankind was never meant to mourn their children.

STARTING OVER AGAIN

I discovered I was pregnant on October 18th, 2022. Unfortunately, news that should have brought nothing but delight brought fear and hesitation. Don't get me wrong, I'm so excited to have another baby, but the fear of losing this one too, is just... I don't think I could do it again. I told Spencer that I wanted to keep it between us, because the more people who know, the more phone calls we have to make explaining what happened should we lose this child. We waited around two weeks until Spencer's mom finally asked, "Is Sarah pregnant?!"

I guess it didn't occur to me that after all my praying, I could be pregnant with... another boy. I've never worried about having another son. I've never thought that two sons would be too much or not enough. But having Kate and then grieving Kate made it so a daughter-sized hole was created in my heart. While we rejoice in the child we have, this news brings in a new wave of grief: Not just for Kate, but for the daughter I made room for but never had and may never have. I didn't want to have to look at her clothes and think of all the beautiful things she'll never pass down to a sister. I didn't want to hear how we should have kept all of Jack's old things when we learned Kate was a girl. I didn't want to say goodbye to this silly idea of manicures and lattes as we talk about college and what boy she's seeing. I didn't want to say goodbye to the dream of mama–daughter dates and matching outfits and the friend who'll last a lifetime. In the days following that call from my doctor, I felt low. I felt lost. I felt awful. I wrote a letter to my son telling him how much I loved him and that I wished I wasn't sad. I told him how he deserved a mother who would celebrate him for everything he is, and not be disappointed for what he wasn't. I told him I'd try to get myself together and be happy because he deserved to be treated like the perfect gift from God that he was. I felt an overwhelming guilt for harboring

70

this dream for a daughter, only to be handed a boy who deserved the same.

But then I saw him. All three ounces of him. Happy, healthy, wiggly, kicking baby boy in the ultrasound. Then the dream changed. I get to be a boy-mom. Instead of lattes and manicures, we'll play video games and watch football. I'll get to watch Jack take on the role of big brother and watch as their friendship develops. I get the dream of having a three and six-year-old wrestling over the last yogurt, watching my fifteen-year-old ask the eighteen-year-old for dating advice, and one day watching them be each other's best man at their weddings. We bought a book entitled "Just Me and My Little Brother," which we've already read to Jack numerous times. After a while, the thought of giving away Kate's clothes no longer scared me the same way. What I could only describe as a God-given sense of peace came over me and this new beautiful boy. I can do this.

BOUNCY BALL STRIKES AGAIN

Despite the new peace I had, triggers of grief and fear still showed up. The ball never stops bouncing. At one of my routine appointments the doctor tried to find the heartbeat with the doppler and was unable to. Considering how early I was in my pregnancy, it's a pretty common problem that the baby's heart just isn't big enough. But in the minutes following (felt like hours) that we waited for the doctor to return with the portable ultrasound machine, a panic came over me. "What if the baby is gone? What if this is it? What if I have to be induced right now to deliver another stillborn baby? Or worse? What if they have to perform a D&C? I don't know that I could handle that." Thankfully after a few minutes, the doctor came back with the ultrasound machine and was able to distinctly see his heart beating away.

Before the holidays, I'd decided that I wanted to honor Kate in some way, so in our hearts, she could be with us on Christmas day. Spencer decided an ornament would be a good idea, so I bought a custom ornament with baby footprints on it reading:

"Kate Amelia

05.28.2022

Sleep in Heavenly Peace"

I didn't anticipate that this small acrylic ornament would forever change how I heard one of my favorite Christmas carols. On Christmas Eve, we went to Spencer's parents' church for a candlelit service. Among the worship songs and carols they sang was "Silent Night." This one line that never really meant much to me overwhelmed me. I thought of our girl, laying cold in my arms, how she was so pure, how she never even had a chance to be welcomed by the world. I thought of our Savior holding my sweet child and taking better care of her than I ever could. I thought of the peace and joy that she must be experiencing in the arms of Jesus. And then I thought of the hole in my heart where my daughter once lay. In the middle of service, I broke down in tears in Spencer's arms as our parents came, one by one, to console me.

REMINDERS OF YOU

With this new pregnancy, our baby boy expected in June 2023, I made the decision to keep the pregnancy fairly quiet (which for millennials, means it wasn't on Instagram or Facebook). Keeping this secret is definitely strange. I feel like having it so personal makes it almost feel like it's not really happening, and I would forget that I was even pregnant... until recently. I started showing. I would look at myself in the mirror and chide myself for gaining weight until I processed that I'm carrying a baby. I didn't let go, I am pregnant. With child. In the family way. All that jazz.

Around the holidays, I'd gotten some Christmas money to spoil myself and I decided to buy some new maternity dresses. When they arrived, I did a little fashion show for myself with my new dresses and I couldn't help but notice how beautiful and round my pregnant belly was. I'm normally in over-sized tee shirts and hoodies, so I don't really notice that often. I was so full of emotion I started to cry. This didn't happen just once, but every time I tried on a new maternity dress. I wish I could say that what I was feeling was joy. Overwhelming, incandescent joy for my precious son... but instead it was grief. Returned. The disgusting painful stabbing in my chest reminding me that the last time I had this belly, there was a baby girl inside. A girl who would never smile at her parents, who would never cry, who was gone before she even arrived. Oh, my sweet son, I rejoice for you and I praise God for you. But while I celebrate your health and the boy I will meet soon, I grieve the sister you won't get to meet. I grieve the daughter your dad and I lost.

I feel you kicking as I'm typing this and I feel like you're telling me, "It's okay, Mama." I wish there was a way for me to clearly and eloquently explain to you that my grief doesn't mean I love you any less. I adore you, all ten ounces of you! I so look forward to holding you and smothering you with affection and watching you and Jack grow up and beat the tar out of each other (assuming you boys are anything like your dad and uncles). I have so much joy, excitement, anticipation, and eagerness when I think of you... it's just that right now, being pregnant also reminds me of her, and the pain, fear, and hopelessness that your dad and I felt when we lost her.

My greatest fear is that one day you'll read this and think you weren't wanted, or weren't important. My son, there is nothing farther from the truth. You are so deeply loved, wanted, and so, so important.

Since I last wrote, I've finally been able to look at my pregnant belly with nothing but excitement and eagerness to meet my sweet, sweet son.

REDECORATING AND REGRETS

I think one of the hardest parts of this chapter in life is because it's so in-between—baby boy is here but he's not here yet—is that it's easy to get forgetful. All day today, I'd watch Jack playing with his cars, or observing a baby at church, or running around and I would get so excited: "I can't wait to have another boy." But part of the transition from one kiddo to two is that we're planning to convert the guest room into a playroom, which means measuring everything, finding a pull-out couch that will fit our narrow doorways, and picturing where everything could end up. In my measuring and calculating, I looked back online to find the tummy time mat that we were gifted for Kate, as it's in storage and not as easily accessible (thank you, internet!) I was imagining where it would be—nursery or playroom? As my mind began to wander, I caught myself thinking, "I could put it here, so that way, Jack can be playing in his teepee over there and Katie can have tummy time." I can't express the sick guilt that came over me.

I feel so remorseful for the way I feel, the things I think, how I keep mixing up these two children in the in-between time. I know once he's here, everything will be different. I only had dreams of a life with Kate, whereas I will have reality with our new son. I feel so racked with guilt sometimes that I feel like, even though he's not even born yet, I already owe him a pony. TWO ponies. And a convertible. Sometimes, I catch myself thinking how unfair it is to be the child that comes after a stillbirth. You're loved and wanted and precious, but you'll never replace the one that was lost.

I think this whole upstairs conversion we're hoping to do is just a bit of "start-over-ness" that I'm hoping for. We've been planning to move to Idaho since before Kate was even conceived, but delay after delay after hope after hope, and we're still not there. Of course, we trust God's infinite wisdom and timing, and it'll happen when it happens, but maybe the thought of moving better prepares me for a life post-Kate. Maybe that's why we've got the sudden urge to redecorate and reorganize and reconfigure. (That and oh-my-word! Have I told you how many toys Jack got for Christmas?!)

I'm actually learning that it's a really common thing, especially for people with ADHD, to want to reorganize your space in times of change. I remember after a fairly significant break-up, I got a new bed-frame, painted my room, and flipped everything about 180 degrees. In that same vein of thought, it's almost surprising that I didn't try to do this sooner. Maybe I've finally accepted that she cannot be replaced. Maybe I'm ready to move forward in life with two sons and the memory of my daughter. Maybe I'm begging my in-laws and parents to STOP BUYING TOYS FOR JACK—HE HAS ENOUGH.

*Authors Note:

After all the stressing about trying to figure out how to configure the extra room and convert it into the playroom of our dreams, it just makes sense that NONE of it would come to fruition. Life is chaos. We're just rolling with it.

ANNIVERSARIES AND ANNOUNCEMENTS

One of my fellow mamas in this miserable club posted a beautiful sentiment about her daughter on the one-year anniversary of her death. This baby was four days old, and declared brain dead, and the family made the heartbreaking decision to take her off life support and allow her to join her savior. The post was so sweet and full of joy, declaring that today is her "life" anniversary, the day she began life in heaven and it was so inspirational and positive that it made me want to chuck my phone across the room.

Now, this mama is a dear friend of mine, and I celebrate the healing and faithfulness that she's experienced and that she's putting out into the world, but man, I don't feel that way today. It's something to say, "She'll never know fear, or pain, or heartache—only Jesus," and it's wonderful to hear, but I would claw her out of the arms of God if I could hold her in my own. Even with the promise of this beautiful, completely healthy new baby boy, I still want my daughter back.

If you've got a weak stomach, skip this paragraph. I look at the pictures and one video we have of our daughter, already gone, already cold. She was already decaying, the white film all over her tiny little body, and her little lips already rubbed raw from the womb. They couldn't bathe her without risking breaking the skin and making it even more traumatizing for us. I look at my friend's post, and I see a fresh, alive baby, and envy her (what?!) because she got to see what her baby looked like after a bath... she got to hold a warm baby in her arms and feel that tiny heartbeat against her chest.

This beautiful dedication to her daughter came the day before we announced our pregnancy, (absolutely terrible timing on our part, but I had to announce it before I sent out baby shower invites). There was so much weight on this announcement that I called my mom earlier to ask, "Am I ready to announce this? What am I waiting for?" and I think I finally know the answer: I was waiting for the light to turn green. Ever done that? Been stuck at a stop sign for about five-minutes only to realize that you were waiting for the light (that doesn't exist) to turn green. That's how life feels sometimes. You're at a place and you're waiting for a great sign from God, the universe, or Oprah to "do the thing" without processing that sign will never come. The universe is a bunch of matter, Oprah has better things to do, and while God cares greatly about us, he's given us complete free will. It's entirely dependent on the US to make that decision, make that call, or in our case, post that picture to Instagram.

UGLY IN-BETWEEN

When Kate passed away, Spencer and I felt like we were completely cheated out of the newborn experience, and we were. Even when Jack was a newborn, we were separated due to the pandemic, and he was in the NICU for several days, and we just weren't given that opportunity to have a "normal" birthing experience. I recently saw a video of a woman who'd experienced something similar to us: she'd given birth to a daughter who was born unable to breathe and ended up passing away the next day. She shared about how years later she'd cried tears of joy when she heard her son cry once he was born, expressing that she'd never gotten to hear her daughter cry. I feel like I'm there, but instead of the happy ending, I'm in the ugly in-between.

Tomorrow isn't promised, we know this. We hear it all the time, I've been hearing since my early childhood how "we're in the end times." We won't know until Gabriel blows his horn, but my point is, anything can happen. In this ugly in-between, I've already lost Kate, our sweet, tiny girl, but I haven't yet gained our newborn son. There is a chance, although it's miniscule, that we could lose him too. And that fear, that discouragement, that unsettling feeling seems normal for someone in my position, right? Then why do I feel so guilty? Jack. I love him. I love my rambunctious, stubborn, fiercely independent three-year-old. "Why can't you just be happy with what you have, instead of being selfish and wanting more children?" a voice in my head crows. I have no answer. So in the ugly in-between, we have grief, fear, discouragement, and now guilt. Fabulous.

What happens when I hold this boy in my arms, and once he grows out of them, my arms feel empty again? Is it selfish to want more children? Or is it simply that I want what I lost? What if when I see his beautiful face, the bouncy ball hits the wall, and I'm in a wave of grief, unable to process the perfect miracle before me? What if I go the next three months, overcoming my fears and clinging to joy, only for his heart to stop beating before I get to hear him cry?

I keep saying that this is probably the easiest pregnancy I've had so far. With Jack, I had no idea what was happening. With Kate, I was miserably sick the whole time. This time, I have energy, I'm in a good mood (mostly) and Jack is old enough to help take care of himself a little bit more. The only thing dampening this pregnancy is the dark cloud of fear over my head. It's crazy to think there was ever a day where I still had hope that Kate would survive, considering how deeply I've been impacted by her death. I wish I could experience that again: the confidence that my child will survive, that there will be a happy ending to this pregnancy. What if that pregnancy had never happened? What if I didn't have that fear over my head? Would I look at this boy with confidence?

Would I have a dark cloud? Would I be stuck in this ugly in-between?

VALUE

"So far baby boy is super healthy with just a little swelling in his kidney (which could be completely normal), so the docs will be keeping an eye on it. I'm in the doctor's office every two weeks right now and soon it'll be every week!

"As of tomorrow, I will be twenty-seven (!!!) weeks, and it brings up some very oddly comforting statistics. I think, especially after losing Kate, my mom-brain is literally only thinking of survival rates. While the risk of stillbirth at full term is 1/100 (crazy high!), we know that if a little boy decided to try to make his entrance early, he has a 9/10 chance of survival.

"This brought on an interesting conversation for Spencer and I the other day. Lately I've had this nagging fear of losing this new boy or Jack, and how I feel like they define my value as a human being. I told him that I feel like I'm less valuable to the family than our children (i.e., Jack and this boy & any future kiddos), as if my contribution to this family is our children, and without them I have no value. To which he responded so calmly and gently, that I am more valuable to him than our children, "and even if it were true, that you held less value to me and our families than Jack, you would still be valuable."

Now why bring this up?

Number 1: To be candid about how I'm doing. (Plus, I always love getting a chance to share Spencer's bits of wisdom & love)

Number 2: because I feel like a lot of moms might be in this boat with me, feeling like their worth is bound up in their children, but just as my husband comforted me, I want to comfort you. You are valuable. Not because you have a husband or children, but because you're created in God's image. You. Are. Valuable."

—From Sarah's Instagram

REJOICE! REJOICE!

"This pregnancy has been... different.

"I feel like it resembles both prior pregnancies and neither of them at the same time. But I will say this pregnancy has been the most emotionally draining. I've not cried more, or been more scared, or depressed or stressed than I have during this pregnancy. I've experienced spiritual warfare, pregnancy mood swings, and challenge after challenge after challenge. But, like the wonderful God he is, he reminds us daily that he WILL provide, that he WILL comfort, and he IS with us. Even as I cry and scream, this tiny boy in my belly kicks and wiggles, reminding me that there is so much to be thankful for."

—From Sarah's Instagram

I feel like in the last few months, I've used the words "spiritual warfare" so much that they've lost all meaning. But that's the only thing that I think would explain the constant beating down by life and everything that's happened. You know what I'm talking about if you've ever had a chapter where you've contemplated burning the house down because, worst case scenario, you end up in a padded cell with no responsibilities and three square meals a day (for legal reasons, this is a joke. Do not burn your house down.) But the last few months have been just like that. Starts with one thing, and then another, and then it opens up a can of worms of a million smaller things that happen, and you're left thinking, "Is this real life?"

Paul writes in Philippians 2 that we should do all things without grumbling. Unfortunately, we spent a good amount of time grumbling and complaining, asking, "Why us?" and really dwelling on the nasty, sucky, garbage dump of a situation we were in.

Slowly but surely, though, God has gently pressed on our hearts to rejoice. Rejoice that in this chapter, God has provided what we've needed. Rejoice that we have a beautiful, kind, wonderful, if rambunctious, three year old. Rejoice that our tiny boy is completely healthy and due to be induced in just shy of 6 weeks. Rejoice that we've been granted wisdom to plan ahead. Rejoice that in all of the frustration, our marriage has remained strong. Rejoice that we have a God who loves us so deeply that he is right there with us in the muck and yuck as we try to crawl through to the other side. Rejoice that there IS an "other side."

I told someone earlier, "You know, it seems like someone down there doesn't want us to rejoice. But you know, my husband and I are pretty stubborn. We're going to rejoice anyway."

BUZZER MALFUNCTION

One thing that I anticipated feeling a lot deeper and a lot more painful was going through a tote of the clothes we had for Kate. I went in, looking for any gender-neutral clothes or hand-me-downs from Jack to take out for the baby boy. I anticipated crying, heart aching, and all in all, grief. It felt, however, so perfunctory. Just another chore.

"Yay, I loved that Johnny Cash shirt."

"I guess this could be for a boy."

"Oh, these pants could definitely work with that onesie I bought."

It a little bit felt like my grief box was broken. In fact, it has felt that way for a while. The bouncy ball hasn't hit the button, or maybe it has and the buzzer is just... not going off? Does it mean that I didn't love her as much as I thought I did? Does it mean that I'll never cry about it again? Am I a horrible person? What kind of mother DOESN'T cry over her deceased daughter's clothes? Has the ball just... stopped?

I'm not an anomaly. I know that. I know that any person I ask would say that "it's normal" and that it'll hit me again someday, but maybe, the buzzer won't be as loud anymore. I half expected to be breaking down sobbing with her blanket once a week for the rest of my life. No one grieves at 100% capacity for 100% of the time. Not the mom who lost her two babies to miscarriage, not the mom who lost her son in an accident at eighteen months old, not the mom who lost her son at twenty-seven to a drug overdose. No one expects us to grieve at 100% forever. Honestly, we'd be pretty miserable people to be around if we did. I heard a Ted Talk from Norma McInerny, how she speaks about her late husband as if he's still there. How grief isn't something we "move on" from, it's something we "move forward" with. By celebrating her new marriage, she's not forgetting the husband she lost, she's moving forward in life, with the love and memory of her late husband in hand. The space between our moments of grief isn't wrong, or neglectful. It's our life; it's us moving forward.

As I write this, I feel God reminding me that even though it wasn't brought on by clothes, or a picture, or anything directly related to my daughter, the buzzer did go off recently. My closest girlfriend had her first child, and instead of a natural, drug-free delivery like she wanted, she was forced to have an emergency cesarean after around thirty hours of unsuccessful laboring, which was both terrifying and painful. When I got the news that she and her daughter were okay, I began to weep. It was grief that my friend had to endure something so scary, (and I wasn't able to be there for her), grief that she didn't get the natural delivery she wanted, and overwhelming relief that her daughter not only survived but was thriving. It may not have had anything to do with Kate, but Kate was there in my heart. Kate was with me, grieving for the smooth delivery that neither I nor my best friend got, Kate was with me, rejoicing that Hazel got to meet her mother and father, go home and start her life.

There is no quota for grieving parents, no requirement for what your grief should look like. No one is ever going to look at you and say, "Okay, did you full on break down sobbing in the middle of Target at least twice this year? No? Okay, turn in your 'Bereaved Parent' badge." There is no one way to grieve. Grief is so weird and so different for so many people, the only thing we really need to know is that God grieves with us and we are never alone in our grief (Psalm 34:18).

*Author's Note:

If you find your buzzer is broken and won't stop buzzing, I urge you to talk to a counselor or a pastor. This could be a sign of chronic depression or post-traumatic stress disorder. There is no shame in seeking help.

OPENING THE FLOODGATES

As I write this, I am thirty-four weeks pregnant and less than five weeks away from our induction date with our baby boy. I have been nesting and cleaning like a mad woman, so when my in-laws offered to watch Jack the other day, I was beyond ready to take on as much as I possibly could. After I'd cleaned Jack's room, cleaned the guest room, and put away three loads of laundry, I decided to sit outside with Spencer to give my achy body a rest. "How's my wife today?" I answered, explaining in detail all that I'd gotten done, all that I had left to do and explained that I felt very accomplished. I could have easily anticipated his next set of questions, but I did not anticipate anything that followed. "How's my baby boy? Is he moving a lot today?" I quickly realized that in my cleaning mayhem that I hadn't felt him move all day. I explained that I hadn't felt him move, but that was likely because of how much I'd been working, but then a thought popped into my mind that I wish never had: What if he's dead? Just like that, the can of worms was opened, the seal was broken, and the floodgates had been opened. That quick thought would be a recurring thought and fear that I'd face for the following two weeks and most likely will continue to face until he's in my arms. I began sobbing and panicking. I immediately ran inside to grab our mini-doppler (thank God for Facebook marketplace) and began searching for his heartbeat. After a moment of looking, 155bpm. Alive. Healthy. Safe... for now.

It's happened a few times since; When I've just woken up, come back from a walk, or finished an invigorating chore. It doesn't even really make it easier when he kicks and reminds me that he's still here. It tells me that he's alive right now, and he'll most likely be alive for the next twenty-four hours. I'd heard before that we all have about four minutes to live but the clock resets every time we take a breath. As ridiculous as that sounds, that's how it's been working in my head. Every kick just resets the clock to another twenty-four hours. I wish I could convince myself that nothing is going to happen, that he'll be safe, but I remember that we had all the confidence in the world that our Kate would make it home.

I feel like these last few weeks, the grief is just background noise, ever-present but I'm able to function through it for the most part. There are the not-so-subtle reminders, the fact that I am now being seen twice a week at the doctor's office, and then there are the in-your-face nightmares that I've been having almost every night. Last night, it was two-fold. The first part, that I began bleeding and no one took my concern seriously. Once I was finally admitted to the hospital, they performed an emergency cesarean and out popped a six-month-old-looking baby boy. The second, from the time I took him home, people were trying to steal him from me, and what's worse, I kept calling him "her." The other night it was even less subtle, I dreamt I'd had another stillbirth.

I'd like to end this chapter with an uplifting remark, but honestly, I think I'm in the trenches now. I feel like I'm army crawling through the mud and muck of this last month of pregnancy, filled with both hope and fear, discouragement and excitement, grief and joy.

MISPLACED GRIEF

For the last week, I've probably had about twelve thousand (more like two) complete meltdowns over very very small things, often allowing my temper to get the best of me and my suddenly very short fuse. The first "event" was on Mother's Day. I went into Target to make a gift card exchange. I'd just read that if I get a gift card for a specialty location, I can transfer the balance to a Target gift card. Rad! Only, not rad! Because wherever I read that wasn't credible, as that is NOT Target's policy, as was told to me by the very concerned customer service agents. In my short-fused emotional tirade, I slammed my hand down on the counter, briskly walked away, and flipped off the building as I got into the car, and was rightfully scolded by my husband for my EXTREMELY childish behavior. I proceeded to cry the entire drive home and then went online to report them, saying that the customer service team was downright awful (they weren't, I was, and I have every intention of giving them raving reviews for the next ten thousand surveys I receive).

All of this rage came to a head the moment I laid eyes on Kate's little shelf. I looked at her ultrasound, her footprints, the ceramic mold of her hand and the sobs came so much harder. I was lashing out at everything else because of my misplaced grief. I'd subconsciously chosen not to grieve for Kate on my first Mother's Day since her death, and chose instead to rage about Target's return policy. I ran upstairs and proceeded to cry my eyes out for a good hour, and then slept. I woke up feeling so foolish and embarrassed at my misplaced grief.

The second time was this afternoon. I had gone to the OBGYN for a non-stress test and had scheduled some more appointments while I was there. When I went home, I logged onto my account with the hospital and tried to transpose all of my appointments into my planner like I do any time I set an appointment.

Only this time, my induction date was missing. I didn't understand why. I tried calling my OB and was put on hold for about ten minutes. I'm already frustrated. I call the hospital where I'm to deliver, and the receptionist says, "Doesn't look like you have that appointment set." I am now frustrated and stressed. I call my OB once again to try to get ahold of someone, and to make a long story short, about fifteen calls, several text messages, an email to my doctor and a full-blown meltdown later, my appointment is right where it's supposed to be.

The problem here was two-fold. First, I'm not supposed to have access to see when my induction is on my account, so me seeing it previously was simply a glitch. Then, the receptionist, who told me that my appointment wasn't set, failed to tell me that she didn't have access to view appointments further than two weeks in the future. Ugh. My very kind nurse called me to tell me everything was okay, the appointment never went off the books and this was just a big misunderstanding.

I realized what was happening on one of the many phone calls I'd made to my mom. She'd said that even if it had gotten canceled, we could easily reschedule for the same day and time. My response was, "What if they can't do it then? If he's not born early, he's going to die!" and then it hit me. I wasn't crying about a miscommunication or misunder-standing or even poor customer service. I was crying because of an irrational grief-based fear that my son would die if I didn't get him out on time. It was a thought I'd had a lot following Kate's passing, that I could've prevented her death if I'd miraculously known to induce early. Of course, no one could have known that, but the thought remains. "What if I'd tried harder to induce labor naturally? What if I'd pushed to induce early like I'd wanted to?"

I'm reminded that even if we had given birth on time, she still would have gone a while without oxygen and likely wouldn't have made it more than a few days anyway. The hard thing about life is that most of the time, we're not given any indication as to when it can end. So even with my induction date, the prenatal vitamins, the extra appointments, and the extra care I've been taking, I could still lose him like I lost Kate almost a year ago...

MONTHS LATER...

HIS BEAUTIFUL VOICE

It's been several months since I've written anything. A few months ago, after my last entry, I was told that I was at risk for pre-eclampsia. At that point, they'd informed me that due to this diagnosis and the already high-risk pregnancy, if I desired, I could induce early, but only at the third nearest hospital, about two hours away, (versus the second nearest, with the NICU, where we'd planned to deliver, 45 minutes away.) We decided to wait until our original induction date, June 22nd, so we could be in the hospital with the NICU.

On June 3rd, 2023, while Spencer was at work at his weekend job, Jack was with his nana, giving me the morning off. I chose to get a mani/pedi and get a latte and I'd gone home to take a nap and do some chores. As I tried to lay down to sleep, I was having fairly painful heart palpitations that scared me. I called my

OB's office and spoke to the on-call doctor. I told him my history and my symptoms and he didn't seem alarmed; even though my blood pressure had peaked, it was still in a healthy range. He reminded me again of the offer to induce early, but I told him we were unable to deliver at the other hospital. We needed the NICU downstairs, just in case. We hung up and he called me back ten minutes later saying that after reviewing my history, he believed that I needed to induce sooner. He said that our desired hospital had an availability immediately, and that if I could get down there that evening, I could be induced. I called Spencer to let him know and I was on the road twenty minutes later.

We'd made arrangements for Jack to stay with Spencer's mom and stepdad for the next night, until Spencer's dad could make it down from Spokane the next day. Spencer's dad would then stay with Jack at our house as long as we were gone, or until my parents were able to make the drive up to Oregon from southern

California. Everything was in place, and we were ready to get the ball rolling.

The evening went smoothly once Spencer and I arrived at the hospital together. I got the pain medication I'd wanted, we watched movies and set off the phone tree, calling family members and letting them know what was happening. We'd gotten a few hours of sleep here and there throughout the night. The next morning I'd told the nurses our story, explaining our loss, explaining our history with Jack's NICU stay, explaining that my only desire was to hear my son cry. I'd never heard my children cry when they were born. Jack couldn't breathe, and Kate was no longer with us. I wanted to hear our son cry.

On June 4th , 2023, at 3:46 p.m., Alexander James "AJ" was born, crying, with the most beautiful voice, I'd ever heard. Spencer and I exchanged remarks, laughing and crying at the same time. "He's crying!" I said. "He's ALIVE," Spencer replied.

YET

When they did their initial check-up on AJ, they found that his breathing was a little irregular and recommended that he stay in the NICU overnight. Well, overnight turned into two nights, then three, then four, then five, and finally seven. Seven days we were told that our son "could go home tomorrow." Despite his gestational age being over thirty-seven weeks, he was considered a preemie, needing extra help learning to suck, breathe, regulate his temperature, et cetera, et cetera. We were given the freedom to come and go as we pleased. Had this been our first child, this would have been a no-brainer to spend every waking moment at the hospital, but we also had our three-year-old to consider. What I never realized was how BADLY it could go.

We'd spent Saturday, Sunday, and Monday, away from home, and decided that on Tuesday, we'd come home to spend a few hours with Jack and Spencer's dad. I came home, so excited to see Jack, who then completely rejected me from the moment I walked in the door. He seemed to be really angry at me, specifically, for leaving him. Devastatingly, Spencer's dad informed us that the ceramic hand and foot moldings of Kate's had been broken by accident while we were gone. Far from destroyed, and completely repairable, the shock hit us hard. To make matters worse, my breastmilk had come in and almost immediately, I'd gotten clogged ducts. I remember taking a shower and sobbing. It felt like my world had fallen apart: losing a part of my daughter, being rejected by my son, fearing for our newborn, and now in the most miserable physical pain. I wish I could say that everything got better so fast, but we were only in the beginning of a very long and miserable week.

As the days went on, we continued to go home for a few hours almost daily to see Jack, and each day I was rejected by Jack. It got to the point where I'd brought Starbucks cake pops and candy to bribe him into spending time with me. The clogged ducts seemed to clear up, though I was still incredibly uncomfortable, and we were seeing the light at the end of the tunnel with AJ. I kept thinking about how painful it was that we were back with the thought, "We can't take our child home." It brought back the thought of the quiet car, where there should be a tiny baby cooing. I struggled to find hope, but God impressed on me the word "yet." It wasn't "I can't take my child home." It was "I can't take him home... yet."

Finally, one week after he was born, we were able to take our sweet son home to meet his brother and to start our lives together as a family of four.

MORE
MONTHS
LATER...

KEEP MOVING FORWARD

The last few months with AJ have been a whirlwind.

Spencer not only got the job opportunity he was hoping for, but a few months after he completed training he was offered a transfer to Boise. We moved just before Christmas. We are loving the snow and sunshine, and happy to finally be in Idaho.

AJ is now over seven months old, close to crawling. He is a very happy, smiley boy. He's eating solid foods and playing and learning how to grab things. He's wearing six to twelve month clothing and lovingly called "chunky monkey."

Jack has returned to his goofy, clingy self and is an excellent big brother to AJ, doting on him with kisses, snuggles, and stuffies. I frequently hear throughout the day, "Mom, AJ wants to snuggle me!" Informing me that I should pick up AJ and place him on Jack's lap. When AJ was much smaller, Jack would sneakily pick him up and move him to the couch, but now, as AJ is much larger, Jack asks for help. Jack got potty trained and attended a semester at a local Christian preschool while we were still in Oregon. He made several friends and a lot of progress in his development. He is now a full-on homeschool kid, eager to learn and be involved in everyday activities.

Kate's hand and foot molds were glued back together. They now sit safely on my nightstand. I've still slept with her blanket every night, except for a few weeks when it was misplaced due to the move. Right now, it's back on my bed waiting for me. The diamond created from her ashes arrived just before Christmas day. It's absolutely beautiful, and yet not at all what I was expecting. The plan is to have the diamond mounted in a simple band to wear on my right hand or around my neck on a chain.

I find myself thinking frequently about my children. I think about what it would be like if all of my children lived: If, instead of losing the first baby, Jack had a twin brother. If Kate survived and we still had AJ. How much fuller our lives would be. How much joy and chaos would fill my every waking moment. I think often about what it would be like to have a little Kate running around with her brothers, and my heart aches at the thought of what could've been. But I sat at dinner last night and I watched. I watched as Spencer was talking to Jack who was eating and then making faces at AJ. I thought to myself, "This is my world." My entire world packed in a tiny booth at a Texas Roadhouse in Nampa.

Spencer and I have decided that we'll try for another baby soon. And, who knows, maybe we'll try for another one after that. I must confess, there's a decent-sized part of me that's worried that we'll lose another one; That the number of children I have in heaven will outweigh the number of children under my roof. I don't know if I could endure that again. Since having AJ, my intrusive thoughts are... dark. I've thought of every way possible I could lose this boy, and on top of that the thought that what if while I'm tending to AJ, something disastrous happens to Jack? I can't tell you how many times I've stared at our baby monitor just to make sure that they're both breathing while they sleep. I heard someone say recently, "Don't worry, they WANT to live." As weird as it sounds, it brought me comfort.

Completely unrelated to grief, I think the biggest thing I've been struggling with lately is trying to feel like a person again. Not just "Mom" but a person. A person with feelings and opinions and a personality and style and interests outside of what organizing system I have for the kid's clothes, and what clever way I can sneak vegetables into my family's meals. I've been sneaking away from time to time to go to the local coffee shop and read my bible, and I've even taken tests to see if I could get into Mensa, (I'm close but I don't qualify right now, but man, wouldn't that be something!). I think as time goes on, I'll start to feel more and more like myself again.

EVEN MORE MONTHS LATER...

PEACE, BY DEFAULT

Alexander James is nearly fifteen months old, crawling, babbling, and absolutely huge.

Jack Leon is four and a half, and convinced he's the boss of the house.

Baby number three is safe in Mama's belly and roughly the size of a lemon.

The day after AJ's first birthday, I discovered I was pregnant. A little surprising, but very joyful indeed. I'm now thirteen weeks, and all signs point to a happy, healthy baby... boy. We aren't one hundred percent certain, but that's the educated guess. We'll find out for certain next week when the results of the chromosome test come back, but I couldn't help but feel a little... bummed. Not the same sadness I felt upon learning about AJ being a boy, but still a small sadness nonetheless. I love and will continue to love this baby, no matter what, but

I think it's just the hope of having a little girl being thwarted... or reliving the grief of losing the chance to raise our daughter.

A few months ago, on what would have been Kate's second birthday, I felt the grief of her loss again. These moments have become pretty few and far between but still very real. I remember breaking down to Spencer, saying, "I just miss her... I just wish she were here." It's definitely strange having more babies after losing babies. I feel I'm expecting another loss around every corner, and yet so emotionally exhausted from active grief that I'm choosing peace by default. I have no idea what the future will bring... what God will bring. I honestly have been more focused on our finances and figuring out the next steps of our life as a family than I have about obsessing over every detail of this pregnancy. It's almost as if the pregnancy and all the worries that would previously accompany it are taking a back seat to everything in front of us. Not because it's not important, on the contrary—this child is very dear and important to me. Not because I'm confident that nothing will go wrong but because I have hope. Because I know that right now, this baby is healthy. Because I have hope that this baby will continue to thrive. Because even if God chooses to take this baby to his eternal home in heaven before I have a chance to meet him, I know that we can pick ourselves up and move forward.

PEACE IN THE STORM

At around fifteen weeks pregnant, we learned that the baby boy growing in my belly was at risk for some health issues. Doctors found a mosaic issue with the Y chromosome, so that left us with a wide variety of potential problems. On the list of what could be wrong, answers range anywhere from absolutely nothing, to severe bone deformities, infertility as an adult, debilitating mental illnesses, or even the inability to survive the pregnancy. As one could imagine, this was incredibly triggering. I was flooded with memories of sitting in the office, hoping only to receive ultrasound photos of my daughter, and then hearing, "Most people consider an abortion."

I honestly don't remember much about that day, except for crying my eyes out in bed, trying to sleep. Many bouts of sobbing have happened since then. This whole chapter of life has brought back so many memories of Kate and the pain along with it. One of the conversations I had with the genetic counselor was, "Is there a chance that, if my husband and I try to conceive again, we would run into the same situation?" While she assured me that this particular genetic defect happens at random, and there's no data to suggest that, given our history, we shouldn't try to conceive again should we want to, I'm still left with doubts. I find myself blaming my womb for not being able to consistently create healthy children...and asking myself if it's worth the risk to try for another baby one day.

This last Sunday at church, I told Spencer I'd been having dreams about having a daughter. He asked me, "Do you want to try again?" I quietly replied, "I don't know if we should." A few moments later, during worship, I turned around and saw a mom holding hands with her young daughter, Kate's age while twirling her around like a ballerina... that was one of the most intense moments of grief I've had in a long time, as I broke down sobbing in the middle of the sanctuary.

Each day, I have more and more faith about this baby growing in my belly and more and more questions about what the future holds. I, do, however, have peace—not delight, or even hope, but peace. Peace, knowing that I can continue to cry and grieve. Peace, knowing that we can survive what comes our way. Peace, knowing that one day we will spend eternity with Christ, AND our children.

My grief journey isn't over. It didn't stop when I had AJ; it won't stop when I have this baby, and it won't stop any time soon. I imagine I'll grieve Kate for the rest of my life. The ball will keep bouncing as the space between grows wider. I can't say that I don't still miss Kate and wish she was here. But I can say that I'm ready to continue forward and share my story.

We're okay, Kate. Rest in the arms of Jesus. You're where you belong.

A LETTER TO MY SONS

My beautiful, wonderful boys.

I'm sure it couldn't have been easy witnessing your parents grieving. It couldn't have been easy to always hear about the sister that didn't make it. I KNOW it's not easy for you to have a mother who's so gosh darned emotional about everything. But let me be absolutely clear:

I am the luckiest mother in the world to have each of you.

Nothing, and nobody can take that away.

You were each hand-picked by God to be my children, and for that, I rejoice.

Jack and AJ: my heart is so full of love and pride for you both. I'm constantly amazed at your relationship, this sibling connection that seems so strong for two boys so young. I find myself eagerly looking forward to the kind of shenanigans you boys will get into as you grow older. Water gun fights in the backyard, wrestling in the living room, even the thought of you boys, as young adults, playing pranks on us. I look forward to watching you boys each becoming the other's confidante, telling secrets, asking advice, and even plotting ways to get us to get pizza and ice cream. I cannot wait until your little brother comes along and can join in on the chaos.

Lucas: I am so thankful for every moment with you in my belly. Stay healthy and keep fighting, little one. I can't wait to hold you in my arms.

I am so thankful to be your mother, and no amount of grief or stress could take that away. I love you as big as the sky.

Love,
Mama
P.S.
Remember:
Gentle Hands
Listening Ears
& Stinky Feet

ABOUT THE AUTHOR

Sarah Boulton is a wife and mother of a growing family. She has a self-proclaimed "gift of gab," and frequently got in trouble at school and work for being very chatty. She dreams of one day homesteading on a large acreage in Tennessee, where she can continue to homeschool her children. Sarah Boulton is a devout Christian and credits Christ for every good thing in her life.